The Dream Journal

one spirit

The Dream Journal

First published in the USA in 2008 by One Spirit
Bertelsmann Direct North America, Inc.
One Penn Plaza
250 West 34 Street
New York, NY 10119

Created by One Spirit and Duncan Baird Publishers
Designed by Duncan Baird Publishers

ISBN:978-1-84483-753-3

10 9 8 7 6 5 4 3 2 1

Typeset in Filosofia
Cover reproduction by Imagewrite, UK
Printed in Thailand by Imago

INTRODUCTION
by David Fontana

I cannot remember a time when I have not been interested in dreams. As a child, they were an entry into a magic world which convinced me that there was more to existence than the commonplace experiences of daily life. When I talked to my young friends, I found they enjoyed the same fascination with this inner world, and we often shared with each other our nighttime adventures (most of which probably lost nothing in the telling), spanning the gamut from fairy-tale happenings in which animals talked and wishes were granted, to the most blood-curdling and terrifying of nightmares. Probably I was lucky, in that most of my dreams were of the pleasant kind, taking me deeper and deeper into what I came to recognize in later years as the mysteries of my unconscious.

The varied richness of my dream life was such that even when I took up the study of psychology in my student days, nothing shook my conviction that dreams are a vital part of our mental life, carrying messages that help to reveal our hidden hopes and fears, and sometimes providing us with guidance and advice unthought of by the conscious, waking mind. I discovered the work of Freud and Jung and learned how dreams can help the psychotherapist understand the client's problems, and give valuable clues on what needs to be done in order to put these problems right.

Later, studying Buddhism, Hinduism, and other Eastern traditions, I discovered the great importance that other cultures attach to dreaming, even seeing it as providing insights into what happens to consciousness after physical death. I learned that it is possible increasingly to take control of one's dreaming, to remember dreams in great detail upon waking, to influence the content of dreams, and even to dream consciously (so-called "lucid dreaming"), so that the mind can determine the course of one's dream adventures, and can actively seek the guidance and wisdom for which it longs.

The more I've studied dreaming, the more I recognize the inadequacy of suggestions by some scientists that dreaming is merely analogous to a computer dumping unwanted data at the end of the working day. Nevertheless, it is important to recognize the advances that science has made in helping us understand, if not the cause and purpose of dreams, at least some of the mechanisms behind them. As a result of these advances we know that everyone, from very young babies to the elderly, appears to dream every night, and those who claim not to do so are simply unable, unless aroused when changes in brain function indicate that dreaming is taking place, to remember their dreams. Modern researchers also teach us that dreaming appears to be important to our psychological health; that no single theory can account for the richness and variety of dreams, that many creative ideas come through dreams, that telepathy, clairvoyance, and even perhaps precognition appear to feature in some dreams, and that dreams may give hints of a higher, spiritual aspect of our mental lives.

My own experiences at running dream workshops and using dreams as an aid toward psychological understanding have shown me, in addition, that many people find that dreaming is great fun. Dreams break all the laws of waking life. In dreams, the elderly can become young again, and the young can become old. The failures and disappointments of waking life can be remedied. Flying and time travel become not only possible but absurdly easy. New dimensions of experience and of feeling and knowing open up effortlessly. People and objects change shape as if under the spell of an enchanter, and sometimes there are glimpses of scenes and places that resemble paradise. So although I hope you may learn more about yourself from this Dream Journal, I hope above all else that you will find it fun, and that it will help to enrich your journeyings into the strange, undiscovered country that beckons to us each nightfall.

DAVID FONTANA

Record your dreams in this journal as soon as possible after waking—keep it by your bedside. Space has been left not only for the dreams themselves but also for your interpretations (including any symbols you can identify) and for your notes on their various moods.

Every so often we have included a "Cues and Connections" page. This is an opportunity for you to track the progress of your dream life generally. You can use this page to trace connections between dreams. Also, you can write down, any evening, the topics you would like to dream about: if you read what you have written and hold the words in your mind just before you fall asleep, you have a good chance of prompting a dream on that subject.

At the back of the book is an A-to-Z directory of common dream symbols to help you to interpret your dreams.

DATE

_____

DREAM

_____

_____

_____

_____

_____

_____

SYMBOLS

_____

_____

_____

_____

MOOD

_____

_____

INTERPRETATION

_____

_____

_____

_____

_____

_____

_____

DATE

_____

DREAM

_____
_____
_____
_____
_____
_____

SYMBOLS

_____
_____
_____
_____

MOOD

_____
_____

INTERPRETATION

_____
_____
_____
_____
_____
_____
_____

DATE

_____

DREAM

_____

_____

_____

_____

_____

_____

SYMBOLS

_____

_____

_____

_____

MOOD

_____

_____

INTERPRETATION

_____

_____

_____

_____

_____

_____

_____

DATE

_____

DREAM

_____

_____

_____

_____

_____

_____

SYMBOLS

_____

_____

_____

_____

MOOD

_____

_____

INTERPRETATION

_____

_____

_____

_____

_____

_____

_____

DATE

_____

DREAM

_____

_____

_____

_____

_____

_____

SYMBOLS

_____

_____

_____

_____

MOOD

_____

_____

INTERPRETATION

_____

_____

_____

_____

_____

_____

_____

DATE

_____

DREAM

_____

_____

_____

_____

_____

_____

SYMBOLS

_____

_____

_____

_____

MOOD

_____

_____

INTERPRETATION

_____

_____

_____

_____

_____

_____

_____

DATE

_____

DREAM

_____

_____

_____

_____

_____

_____

SYMBOLS

_____

_____

_____

_____

MOOD

_____

_____

INTERPRETATION

_____

_____

_____

_____

_____

_____

_____

DATE
_____

DREAM
_____
_____
_____
_____
_____
_____

SYMBOLS
_____
_____
_____
_____

MOOD
_____
_____

INTERPRETATION
_____
_____
_____
_____
_____
_____
_____

DATE

_____

DREAM

_____

_____

_____

_____

_____

_____

SYMBOLS

_____

_____

_____

_____

MOOD

_____

_____

INTERPRETATION

_____

_____

_____

_____

_____

_____

CUES AND CONNECTIONS

"*A dream which is not interpreted is like a letter which is unread.*"

The Talmud (c.200AD–500AD)

DATE

_____

DREAM

_____

_____

_____

_____

_____

SYMBOLS

_____

_____

_____

MOOD

_____

_____

INTERPRETATION

_____

_____

_____

_____

_____

_____

_____

DATE
_____

DREAM
_____
_____
_____
_____
_____
_____

SYMBOLS
_____
_____
_____
_____

MOOD
_____
_____

INTERPRETATION
_____
_____
_____
_____
_____
_____
_____

DATE

_____

DREAM

_____

_____

_____

_____

_____

SYMBOLS

_____

_____

_____

MOOD

_____

_____

INTERPRETATION

_____

_____

_____

_____

_____

_____

_____

DATE

DREAM

SYMBOLS

MOOD

INTERPRETATION

DATE

_____

DREAM

_____

_____

_____

_____

_____

_____

SYMBOLS

_____

_____

_____

_____

MOOD

_____

_____

INTERPRETATION

_____

_____

_____

_____

_____

_____

_____

DATE

_____

DREAM

_____
_____
_____
_____
_____
_____

SYMBOLS

_____
_____
_____
_____

MOOD

_____
_____

INTERPRETATION

_____
_____
_____
_____
_____
_____
_____
_____

DATE

_____

DREAM

_____
_____
_____
_____
_____
_____

SYMBOLS

_____
_____
_____
_____

MOOD

_____
_____

INTERPRETATION

_____
_____
_____
_____
_____
_____
_____

DATE

_____

DREAM

_____
_____
_____
_____
_____
_____

SYMBOLS

_____
_____
_____
_____

MOOD

_____
_____

INTERPRETATION

_____
_____
_____
_____
_____
_____
_____

DATE

_____

DREAM

_____

_____

_____

_____

_____

SYMBOLS

_____

_____

_____

MOOD

_____

_____

INTERPRETATION

_____

_____

_____

_____

_____

_____

CUES AND CONNECTIONS

"Dreams are the touchstones of our character."

Henry David Thoreau (1817–1862)

DATE

_____

DREAM

_____

_____

_____

_____

_____

SYMBOLS

_____

_____

_____

_____

MOOD

_____

INTERPRETATION

_____

_____

_____

_____

_____

_____

DATE

DREAM

SYMBOLS

MOOD

INTERPRETATION

DATE

_____

DREAM

_____

_____

_____

_____

_____

_____

SYMBOLS

_____

_____

_____

_____

MOOD

_____

_____

INTERPRETATION

_____

_____

_____

_____

_____

_____

_____

DATE

_____

DREAM

_____

_____

_____

_____

_____

_____

SYMBOLS

_____

_____

_____

_____

MOOD

_____

_____

INTERPRETATION

_____

_____

_____

_____

_____

_____

_____

DATE

_____

DREAM

_____
_____
_____
_____
_____
_____

SYMBOLS

_____
_____
_____
_____

MOOD

_____
_____

INTERPRETATION

_____
_____
_____
_____
_____
_____
_____

DATE
_____

DREAM
_____
_____
_____
_____
_____
_____

SYMBOLS
_____
_____
_____
_____

MOOD
_____
_____

INTERPRETATION
_____
_____
_____
_____
_____
_____
_____

DATE
_____

DREAM
_____
_____
_____
_____
_____
_____

SYMBOLS
_____
_____
_____
_____

MOOD
_____
_____

INTERPRETATION
_____
_____
_____
_____
_____
_____
_____

DATE

_____

DREAM

_____
_____
_____
_____
_____
_____

SYMBOLS

_____
_____
_____
_____

MOOD

_____
_____

INTERPRETATION

_____
_____
_____
_____
_____
_____
_____

DATE

_____

DREAM

_____

_____

_____

_____

_____

_____

SYMBOLS

_____

_____

_____

_____

MOOD

_____

_____

INTERPRETATION

_____

_____

_____

_____

_____

_____

_____

CUES AND CONNECTIONS

" Judge of your natural character
by what you do in your dreams."

Ralph Waldo Emerson (1803–1882)

DATE

_____

DREAM

_____

_____

_____

_____

_____

SYMBOLS

_____

_____

_____

_____

MOOD

_____

_____

INTERPRETATION

_____

_____

_____

_____

_____

_____

DATE

_____

DREAM

_____
_____
_____
_____
_____
_____

SYMBOLS

_____
_____
_____
_____

MOOD

_____
_____

INTERPRETATION

_____
_____
_____
_____
_____
_____
_____

DATE

_____

DREAM

_____
_____
_____
_____
_____
_____

SYMBOLS

_____
_____
_____
_____

MOOD

_____
_____

INTERPRETATION

_____
_____
_____
_____
_____
_____
_____

DATE

_____

DREAM

_____

_____

_____

_____

_____

SYMBOLS

_____

_____

_____

_____

MOOD

_____

_____

INTERPRETATION

_____

_____

_____

_____

_____

_____

DATE

_____

DREAM

_____
_____
_____
_____
_____

SYMBOLS

_____
_____
_____

MOOD

_____
_____

INTERPRETATION

_____
_____
_____
_____
_____
_____

DATE
_____

DREAM
_____
_____
_____
_____
_____
_____

SYMBOLS
_____
_____
_____
_____

MOOD
_____
_____

INTERPRETATION
_____
_____
_____
_____
_____
_____
_____

DATE

_____

DREAM

_____

_____

_____

_____

_____

_____

SYMBOLS

_____

_____

_____

_____

MOOD

_____

_____

INTERPRETATION

_____

_____

_____

_____

_____

_____

_____

DATE

_____

DREAM

_____

_____

_____

_____

_____

_____

SYMBOLS

_____

_____

_____

_____

MOOD

_____

_____

INTERPRETATION

_____

_____

_____

_____

_____

_____

_____

DATE

_____

DREAM

_____

_____

_____

_____

_____

_____

SYMBOLS

_____

_____

_____

_____

MOOD

_____

_____

INTERPRETATION

_____

_____

_____

_____

_____

_____

_____

CUES AND CONNECTIONS

" What a dream shows is the shadow of such wisdom as exists in us, even if during our waking state we may know nothing about it."

Paracelsus (1493–1541)

DATE

_____

DREAM

_____

_____

_____

_____

_____

_____

SYMBOLS

_____

_____

_____

_____

MOOD

_____

_____

INTERPRETATION

_____

_____

_____

_____

_____

_____

_____

DATE

DREAM

SYMBOLS

MOOD

INTERPRETATION

DATE

_____

DREAM

_____

_____

_____

_____

_____

_____

SYMBOLS

_____

_____

_____

_____

MOOD

_____

_____

INTERPRETATION

_____

_____

_____

_____

_____

_____

_____

DATE
_____

DREAM
_____
_____
_____
_____
_____

SYMBOLS
_____
_____
_____
_____

MOOD
_____
_____

INTERPRETATION
_____
_____
_____
_____
_____
_____
_____

DATE

_____

DREAM

_____

_____

_____

_____

_____

_____

SYMBOLS

_____

_____

_____

_____

MOOD

_____

_____

INTERPRETATION

_____

_____

_____

_____

_____

_____

_____

DATE
_____

DREAM
_____
_____
_____
_____
_____
_____

SYMBOLS
_____
_____
_____
_____

MOOD
_____
_____

INTERPRETATION
_____
_____
_____
_____
_____
_____
_____

DATE

_____

DREAM

_____
_____
_____
_____
_____
_____

SYMBOLS

_____
_____
_____
_____

MOOD

_____
_____

INTERPRETATION

_____
_____
_____
_____
_____
_____

DATE

_____

DREAM

_____
_____
_____
_____
_____
_____

SYMBOLS

_____
_____
_____
_____

MOOD

_____
_____

INTERPRETATION

_____
_____
_____
_____
_____
_____
_____

DATE

_____

DREAM

_____

_____

_____

_____

_____

_____

SYMBOLS

_____

_____

_____

_____

MOOD

_____

_____

INTERPRETATION

_____

_____

_____

_____

_____

_____

_____

CUES AND CONNECTIONS

" To accomplish great things, we must dream
as well as act."

Anatole France (1844–1924)

DATE

_____

DREAM

_____

_____

_____

_____

_____

_____

SYMBOLS

_____

_____

_____

MOOD

_____

_____

INTERPRETATION

_____

_____

_____

_____

_____

_____

_____

DATE

_____

DREAM

_____

_____

_____

_____

_____

_____

SYMBOLS

_____

_____

_____

_____

MOOD

_____

_____

INTERPRETATION

_____

_____

_____

_____

_____

_____

_____

_____

DATE

_____

DREAM

_____

_____

_____

_____

_____

_____

SYMBOLS

_____

_____

_____

_____

MOOD

_____

_____

INTERPRETATION

_____

_____

_____

_____

_____

_____

_____

DATE

_____

DREAM

_____

_____

_____

_____

_____

SYMBOLS

_____

_____

_____

MOOD

_____

_____

INTERPRETATION

_____

_____

_____

_____

_____

_____

DATE

_____

DREAM

_____

_____

_____

_____

_____

_____

SYMBOLS

_____

_____

_____

_____

MOOD

_____

_____

INTERPRETATION

_____

_____

_____

_____

_____

_____

_____

DATE

_____

DREAM

_____

_____

_____

_____

_____

SYMBOLS

_____

_____

_____

MOOD

_____

_____

INTERPRETATION

_____

_____

_____

_____

_____

_____

_____

DATE

_____

DREAM

_____

_____

_____

_____

_____

SYMBOLS

_____

_____

_____

MOOD

_____

_____

INTERPRETATION

_____

_____

_____

_____

_____

_____

_____

DATE

_____

DREAM

_____
_____
_____
_____
_____
_____

SYMBOLS

_____
_____
_____
_____

MOOD

_____
_____

INTERPRETATION

_____
_____
_____
_____
_____
_____
_____

DATE

_____

DREAM

_____

_____

_____

_____

_____

_____

SYMBOLS

_____

_____

_____

_____

MOOD

_____

_____

INTERPRETATION

_____

_____

_____

_____

_____

_____

_____

CUES AND CONNECTIONS

" Why does the eye see a thing more clearly in
dreams than the imagination when awake?"

Leonardo da Vinci (1452–1519)

DATE

_____

DREAM

_____

_____

_____

_____

_____

_____

SYMBOLS

_____

_____

_____

_____

MOOD

_____

_____

INTERPRETATION

_____

_____

_____

_____

_____

_____

_____

DATE

_____

DREAM

_____

_____

_____

_____

_____

_____

SYMBOLS

_____

_____

_____

_____

MOOD

_____

_____

INTERPRETATION

_____

_____

_____

_____

_____

_____

_____

DATE

_____

DREAM

_____

_____

_____

_____

_____

_____

SYMBOLS

_____

_____

_____

_____

MOOD

_____

_____

INTERPRETATION

_____

_____

_____

_____

_____

_____

_____

DATE

_____

DREAM

_____
_____
_____
_____
_____
_____

SYMBOLS

_____
_____
_____
_____

MOOD

_____
_____

INTERPRETATION

_____
_____
_____
_____
_____
_____
_____

DATE

_____

DREAM

_____

_____

_____

_____

_____

_____

SYMBOLS

_____

_____

_____

_____

MOOD

_____

_____

INTERPRETATION

_____

_____

_____

_____

_____

_____

_____

DATE

_____

DREAM

_____

_____

_____

_____

_____

_____

SYMBOLS

_____

_____

_____

_____

MOOD

_____

_____

INTERPRETATION

_____

_____

_____

_____

_____

_____

_____

DATE

DREAM

SYMBOLS

MOOD

INTERPRETATION

DATE

DREAM

SYMBOLS

MOOD

INTERPRETATION

DATE

_____

DREAM

_____

_____

_____

_____

_____

_____

SYMBOLS

_____

_____

_____

_____

MOOD

_____

_____

INTERPRETATION

_____

_____

_____

_____

_____

_____

CUES AND CONNECTIONS

" The soul in sleep gives proof of its divine nature."

Cicero (106BC–43BC)

DATE

_____

DREAM

_____

_____

_____

_____

_____

_____

SYMBOLS

_____

_____

_____

_____

MOOD

_____

_____

INTERPRETATION

_____

_____

_____

_____

_____

_____

_____

DATE

DREAM

SYMBOLS

MOOD

INTERPRETATION

DATE

_____

DREAM

_____

_____

_____

_____

_____

_____

SYMBOLS

_____

_____

_____

_____

MOOD

_____

_____

INTERPRETATION

_____

_____

_____

_____

_____

_____

_____

DATE

_____

DREAM

_____

_____

_____

_____

_____

SYMBOLS

_____

_____

_____

_____

MOOD

_____

_____

INTERPRETATION

_____

_____

_____

_____

_____

_____

DATE

_____

DREAM

_____

_____

_____

_____

_____

_____

SYMBOLS

_____

_____

_____

_____

MOOD

_____

_____

INTERPRETATION

_____

_____

_____

_____

_____

_____

_____

_____

DATE
_____

DREAM
_____
_____
_____
_____
_____
_____

SYMBOLS
_____
_____
_____
_____

MOOD
_____
_____

INTERPRETATION
_____
_____
_____
_____
_____
_____
_____

DATE

_____

DREAM

_____

_____

_____

_____

_____

_____

SYMBOLS

_____

_____

_____

_____

MOOD

_____

_____

INTERPRETATION

_____

_____

_____

_____

_____

_____

_____

DATE

_____

DREAM

_____
_____
_____
_____
_____
_____

SYMBOLS

_____
_____
_____
_____

MOOD

_____
_____

INTERPRETATION

_____
_____
_____
_____
_____
_____
_____

DATE

_____

DREAM

_____

_____

_____

_____

_____

SYMBOLS

_____

_____

_____

MOOD

_____

_____

INTERPRETATION

_____

_____

_____

_____

_____

_____

_____

CUES AND CONNECTIONS

"If the dream is a translation of waking life,
waking life is also a translation of the dream."

René Magritte (1898–1967)

DATE

_____

DREAM

_____

_____

_____

_____

_____

_____

SYMBOLS

_____

_____

_____

_____

MOOD

_____

_____

INTERPRETATION

_____

_____

_____

_____

_____

_____

_____

DATE

_____

DREAM

_____
_____
_____
_____
_____
_____

SYMBOLS

_____
_____
_____
_____

MOOD

_____
_____

INTERPRETATION

_____
_____
_____
_____
_____
_____
_____

DATE

_____

DREAM

_____

_____

_____

_____

_____

_____

SYMBOLS

_____

_____

_____

_____

MOOD

_____

_____

INTERPRETATION

_____

_____

_____

_____

_____

_____

_____

DATE

_____

DREAM

_____
_____
_____
_____
_____
_____

SYMBOLS

_____
_____
_____
_____

MOOD

_____
_____

INTERPRETATION

_____
_____
_____
_____
_____
_____
_____

DATE

_____

DREAM

_____

_____

_____

_____

_____

_____

SYMBOLS

_____

_____

_____

_____

MOOD

_____

_____

INTERPRETATION

_____

_____

_____

_____

_____

_____

_____

DATE

_____

DREAM

_____

_____

_____

_____

_____

_____

SYMBOLS

_____

_____

_____

MOOD

_____

_____

INTERPRETATION

_____

_____

_____

_____

_____

_____

_____

DATE

_____

DREAM

_____

_____

_____

_____

_____

_____

SYMBOLS

_____

_____

_____

_____

MOOD

_____

_____

INTERPRETATION

_____

_____

_____

_____

_____

_____

DATE

_____

DREAM

_____
_____
_____
_____
_____
_____

SYMBOLS

_____
_____
_____
_____

MOOD

_____
_____

INTERPRETATION

_____
_____
_____
_____
_____
_____
_____

DATE

_____

DREAM

_____

_____

_____

_____

_____

_____

SYMBOLS

_____

_____

_____

_____

MOOD

_____

_____

INTERPRETATION

_____

_____

_____

_____

_____

_____

_____

CUES AND CONNECTIONS

" Maybe the wildest dreams are but the needful
preludes of the truth."

Alfred Lord Tennyson (1809–1892)

DATE

_____

DREAM

_____

_____

_____

_____

_____

_____

SYMBOLS

_____

_____

_____

_____

MOOD

_____

_____

INTERPRETATION

_____

_____

_____

_____

_____

_____

_____

DATE

_____

DREAM

_____
_____
_____
_____
_____
_____

SYMBOLS

_____
_____
_____
_____

MOOD

_____
_____

INTERPRETATION

_____
_____
_____
_____
_____
_____
_____

DATE
_____

DREAM
_____
_____
_____
_____
_____
_____

SYMBOLS
_____
_____
_____
_____

MOOD
_____
_____

INTERPRETATION
_____
_____
_____
_____
_____
_____

DATE
_____

DREAM
_____
_____
_____
_____
_____
_____

SYMBOLS
_____
_____
_____
_____

MOOD
_____
_____

INTERPRETATION
_____
_____
_____
_____
_____
_____
_____

DATE

_____

DREAM

_____

_____

_____

_____

_____

SYMBOLS

_____

_____

_____

_____

MOOD

_____

_____

INTERPRETATION

_____

_____

_____

_____

_____

_____

DATE

_____

DREAM

_____
_____
_____
_____
_____
_____

SYMBOLS

_____
_____
_____
_____

MOOD

_____
_____

INTERPRETATION

_____
_____
_____
_____
_____
_____
_____

DATE

_____

DREAM

_____
_____
_____
_____
_____
_____

SYMBOLS

_____
_____
_____
_____

MOOD

_____
_____

INTERPRETATION

_____
_____
_____
_____
_____
_____
_____

DATE
_____

DREAM
_____
_____
_____
_____
_____
_____

SYMBOLS
_____
_____
_____
_____

MOOD
_____
_____

INTERPRETATION
_____
_____
_____
_____
_____
_____
_____

DATE

_____

DREAM

_____
_____
_____
_____
_____
_____

SYMBOLS

_____
_____
_____
_____

MOOD

_____
_____

INTERPRETATION

_____
_____
_____
_____
_____
_____
_____

CUES AND CONNECTIONS

" Those who have compared our life to a dream were right... We sleeping wake, and waking sleep."

Michel de Montaigne (1533–1592)

DATE

_____

DREAM

_____

_____

_____

_____

_____

SYMBOLS

_____

_____

_____

MOOD

_____

_____

INTERPRETATION

_____

_____

_____

_____

_____

_____

_____

DATE

_____

DREAM

_____

_____

_____

_____

_____

_____

SYMBOLS

_____

_____

_____

_____

MOOD

_____

_____

INTERPRETATION

_____

_____

_____

_____

_____

_____

_____

DATE

DREAM

SYMBOLS

MOOD

INTERPRETATION

DATE

_____

DREAM

_____
_____
_____
_____
_____
_____

SYMBOLS

_____
_____
_____
_____

MOOD

_____
_____

INTERPRETATION

_____
_____
_____
_____
_____
_____
_____
_____

DATE

DREAM

SYMBOLS

MOOD

INTERPRETATION

DATE

DREAM

SYMBOLS

MOOD

INTERPRETATION

DATE

_____

DREAM

_____
_____
_____
_____
_____
_____

SYMBOLS

_____
_____
_____
_____

MOOD

_____
_____

INTERPRETATION

_____
_____
_____
_____
_____
_____
_____

DATE

_____

DREAM

_____

_____

_____

_____

_____

_____

SYMBOLS

_____

_____

_____

_____

MOOD

_____

_____

INTERPRETATION

_____

_____

_____

_____

_____

_____

_____

DATE

_____

DREAM

_____

_____

_____

_____

_____

_____

SYMBOLS

_____

_____

_____

_____

MOOD

_____

_____

INTERPRETATION

_____

_____

_____

_____

_____

_____

_____

DATE
_____

DREAM
_____
_____
_____
_____
_____
_____

SYMBOLS
_____
_____
_____
_____

MOOD
_____
_____

INTERPRETATION
_____
_____
_____
_____
_____
_____
_____

A-TO-Z OF DREAM SYMBOLS

Cross-references to other entries in this A-to-Z are shown by **CAPITAL LETTERS**.

ALPHABET To forget the alphabet may show that the dreamer feels frustrated by simple tasks. A letter may be a significant initial.

ANIMAL Animals have different symbolic meanings, often reinforced by tradition and folklore. For example, a bird can represent freedom; a cat, independence; a fish, spirituality; a lion, strength; a monkey, mischief; a snake, male sexuality; a spider, possessiveness; and a wild beast, passion. (See also **ZOO**.)

BED Refuge and safety, or the prospect of sexual adventure.

BIRTH Any representation of birth, not only human birth, signifies new possibilities in the dreamer's life, or the need to nurture the self or others. Also, new ideas or solutions. (See also **PREGNANCY**.)

BOOK Wisdom, intellect, application. Being unable to read or to find a book can suggest that, in waking life, the dreamer is not satisfying his or her intellectual needs. (See also **LIBRARY**.)

BRIDGE A classic symbol of change, linking past and present with the future.

CAR Car journeys may represent free will or voluntary actions performed by the dreamer. For Freud, however, the smooth motion of a car represented the dreamer's progress during psychoanalysis.

CASTLE Security. However, castles can also signify that the dreamer is over-defensive.

CHILDREN Innocence, or a reminder to take into account the physical and emotional needs of others. A demonic or sexually mature child may represent corruption.

CHURCH A church spire can be a symbol of masculinity; or if obscured by clouds it may connote unreachable spiritual goals. To enter a church or a temple symbolizes that the dreamer is searching for spiritual truth or guidance, or simply safety and refuge.

CITY To be lost in a city or town symbolizes the stress of modern-day living on the dreamer. A city with many lights and bright colors shows excitement in the dreamer's life. A walled city suggests possessiveness, or a need for security.

CLOCK The ticking of a clock equates with the beating of the heart. Hence, a racing clock can symbolize emotions running high; a stopped clock, lack of emotion.

CLOTHES Loose, flowing robes, such as those worn by saints and prophets, can represent purity and spirituality; heavy and over-elaborate clothes can stand for earthly vanity or hypocrisy; and clothes that are too tight can indicate the dreamer's desire to escape from current constraints. Being naked can reflect feelings of innocence, sexuality, guilt, or shame, depending on the context.

COLORS
Black – night, mystery, evil, danger, death, resurrection.
White – purity, virginity, mourning, spirituality, light.
Blue – spirituality, intellect, tranquility, distance.
Red – energy, activity, aggression, danger, blood, prohibition.

Yellow – childhood, joyfulness, playfulness, enthusiasm.
Green – nature, the senses, fresh growth, sickness, decay, envy.
Orange – freshness, suppleness, dynamism.
Purple – riches, opulence, luxury, royalty.
Pink – femininity, infancy, gentleness, frivolity, artificiality.
Gold – divinity, wealth, deception, weight, age.
Silver – aspiration, integrity, luck, skill, youth.

COUNTRYSIDE Generally, freedom and relaxation. Its exact
symbolism depends, however, upon the season of the year.
(See also **SEASONS**.)

DEATH The death of a dream character may symbolize finality,
such as the end of a marriage or dismissal from a job. It may also
express the dreamer's fear of losing his or her identity, or a sense
of morality. Funerary paraphernalia, such as tombstones,
obituaries, or even funerals themselves, can reflect the dreamer's
anxiety about the passing of time. Burials may also be metaphors
for feelings associated with repression in waking life.

DEMON / DEVIL Division and disintegration. These malevolent
figures express free-floating or unacknowledged anxieties. They
can also invite the dreamer to face up to unpalatable truths and to
be courageous in the face of adversity.

DRAGON An archetypal symbol of power, dominance, or creative
energy.

EGG A universal symbol of fertility and birth. Newly-hatched eggs
can represent fresh possibilities.

ESCALATOR Ascent on an escalator suggests a move toward goals;
descent signifies losing sight of goals. (See also **STAIRS**.)

EXAMINATION Often the subject of anxiety dreams, especially when the dreamer feels completely unprepared for a test. Examinations are an apt metaphor for concerns about success or failure in life.

EYE The "mirror of the soul." Bright eyes imply a healthy and happy inner life.

FIRE A negative or positive symbol, depending upon its context – fire destroys but it also purges. It can indicate disruptive emotions, such as jealousy and envy, or consciousness and fresh beginnings.

FLOWER Different flowers are charged with different symbolic meanings: for example, a red rose is traditionally a symbol of love; a white lily, of death.

FOOD Eating in a dream can symbolize a lust for life, or both physical and spiritual growth, or the dreamer's sexual appetite. Foods differ in their symbolism: for example, fruit can represent creativity or fertility; milk, kindness; and honey, wealth. Sharing food represents reconciliation.

FOREST Generally a place of fear, or else of sanctuary. If a dreamer is lost in a forest, this may represent that he or she lacks worldly experience or knowledge.

GAME In adult dreams, games are often microcosmic representations of the dreamer's life. A board game might enact the advances and setbacks of recent experience.

GARDEN Analogous with the conscious self, a garden suggests loss of control when it is overgrown, and learning and the fruits of labor when it is well-tended. A walled garden may represent virginity or naivety.

GHOST Alienation from life and fear of death. Some psychologists believe that when dreamers see ghosts in their dreams, they are having out-of-body experiences, or OBEs.

HAIR Strength, vitality, sexuality, and beauty. Cutting hair in a dream, or having your own hair cut, often represents loss; and having your hair shaved off connotes the renunciation of worldly attachments.

HAT Wearing a hat implies the need for concealment, protection, secrecy, or propriety. Tall hats and crowns can symbolize authority by accentuating the wearer's height.

HEART An archetypal symbol of love. The essence of life and center of the emotions. To dream of a broken heart represents loss and sadness. A flowering heart is a symbol of prosperity and growth in love.

HOTEL Impermanence, instability, or feelings of lost identity.

HOUSE Familiar houses connote safety and security. Ruined houses or darkened windows in a house reflect a sense of devastation or desolation.

INTERVIEW A classic anxiety dream. Stern interrogation implies that the dreamer fears authority. Inability to speak suggests that the dreamer has something to hide.

JEWELS Diamonds represent the true self and fidelity; rubies, passion and courage; sapphires, truth and chastity; emeralds, fertility and youthfulness. A hoard of jewels implies greed or the inability to share.

KEY A common metaphor for solving problems or opening up new opportunities.

KNIFE Generally, male sexuality. A knife or dagger can also symbolize excitement, as well as violation or destruction.

LADDER To climb a ladder is a metaphor for progress. A ladder that is too short represents thwarted ambition or desire and can also be a symbol of physical disablement.

LETTER An unopened letter may represent a hidden truth, a missed opportunity, or virginity; a letter that has been opened, a revealed truth, an unnoticed opportunity, or sexual experience. An unexpected letter or package can reflect a new challenge.

LIBRARY Intellect. Being distracted from reading by other people may indicate frustrated intellect or thwarted endeavor. (See also **BOOK**.)

MACHINERY Competent use of machinery can indicate increased personal power. If the dreamer becomes a machine, this may stand for a loss of sensitivity.

MASK This is a potent symbol of the self, and being unable to remove or being forced to wear a mask usually signifies an identity crisis. Such dreams put us in touch with our true natures.

MAZE Being lost in a maze represents frustration. Penetrating a maze to its center enacts the dreamer's descent into the realm of the unconscious.

MIRROR Finding a mirror can symbolize a quest for identity or a need for self-examination. It may also indicate a need to go beyond the superficial in one's thinking.

MONEY Freud believed that money signifies anal fixation. To save or hoard money can represent prudence, avarice, or insecurity.

MOON A female symbol evoking serenity and mystery, the moon also connotes the passing of time and steady progress. A new moon symbolizes new beginnings; a full moon is a symbol of emotional and spiritual completeness.

MOUNTAIN A cloudy mountain peak may represent aspirations that are beyond reach. To dream of climbing a mountain signifies work towards certain goals, with the speed and steepness of the ascent representing the difficulty of achievement. Descending a mountain may connote a defeat or the dreamer's need for safety.

PREGNANCY An indication of something new and important in the dreamer's life. Sometimes a dream of pregnancy can be precognitive or may actually coincide with a baby's conception. (See also **BIRTH**.)

PRIZE Given to the dreamer, a prize represents an actual or desired triumph. Taken away from the dreamer, it can reflect the loss of something that may affect the dreamer's sense of self-worth.

RACE To win a race can suggest that the dreamer recognizes his or her potential in a certain venture. Coming second, third, or last suggests that unrealistic targets have been set, or that the dreamer is struggling to meet his or her goals.

RAIN By enacting the fall of tears, rain may symbolize feelings of sorrow or may even be a portent of a sad occurrence. Rain can also

symbolize spiritual growth in the dreamer's inner life. (See also
WATER.)

RAINBOW Hope, optimism, promise, and forgiveness. Also,
the completion of a physical, emotional, or spiritual journey.

RIVER A river's steady flow signifies wasted time. Standing in a
river suggests clinging to the present; to cross a river represents the
risks involved in changing course.

ROAD An open road often indicates that the dreamer is free and
able to follow a clear path toward a desired goal. A hilly, winding, or
bumpy road can suggest that problems and obstacles will have to be
tackled. An intersection implies that the dreamer must make
a decision.

SCHOOL Learning, competition, fear, nostalgia, or innocence,
depending upon the dream's context. To dream of an overbearing
teacher represents fear or feelings of rebellion toward authority.

SEA A calm sea represents the dreamer's "at-oneness" with the deep
waters of the unconscious. A stormy sea connotes strong emotions
and passions. Drowning in the sea signifies overwhelming desires.

SEASONS Spring symbolizes hope, purity, and new beginnings;
summer, completeness, contentment, and sexual fulfillment;
fall, maturity and the wisdom of old age; winter, death, but also
spirituality and purity. (See also **RAIN** and **SUN**.)

SHAPES Geometrical shapes represent such archetypal concepts as
wholeness and unity (the circle), stability (the square), and the unity
of mind, body, and spirit (the triangle). Spirals are symbols of the
life force, and hence of renewed vitality or birth.

SHOES A female sexual symbol, shoes can represent the dominance of the female aspect of the dreamer's psyche.

SKY Spirituality and contemplation. A clear blue sky denotes pure and transcendent thought; a cloudy or stormy sky shows an inability to think clearly or to perceive important truths.

STAIRS To climb stairs may mean that the dreamer can achieve aspirations; to descend, that goals are difficult. Freud believed that climbing stairs connotes sexual intercourse.
(See also **ESCALATOR**.)

STAR A higher state of consciousness. A star may also signify the dreamer's aspirations.

STATION A conscious decision. The choices available at a train or bus station are analogous with those faced in life – whether to stay or to go, to travel near or far, to make a journey cheaply or expensively. Waiting at a station implies feelings of expectation, which can result in disappointment or elated surprise, depending upon the context of the dream. (See also **TRAIN**.)

STORE Plenty and reward. Stores usually relate to our competence at taking advantage of opportunities. The inability to pay for goods or being unable to reach them on high shelves can suggest that the dreamer's deepest desires are not being fulfilled.

STORM Gathering storm clouds may represent emotions running high. The storm itself may be an emotional crisis or catharsis.

SUN A universal symbol of life and power; an archetype of masculinity and especially of fatherhood. The sun may also stand for consciousness and rationality. Clouds that are obscuring the sun's light may indicate that the dreamer's emotions have overcome his or her intellect.

TEMPLE See **CHURCH**.

TOWN See **CITY**.

TRAIN A male sexual symbol according to Freud, but also a symbol of freedom from responsibility. Missing a train or discovering that you are on the wrong train implies lost opportunities.
(See also **STATION**.)

TREE Stability, domestic security. Also motherhood and, at an archetypal level, the Tree of Life or the Cross of the Crucifixion. A tree with many leaves and/or fruit signifies optimism and plenty.
(See also **FOREST**.)

TUNNEL A Freudian symbol of female sexuality. Tunnels can also imply secrecy and suppressed emotion.

WAR Violent struggles may represent the dreamer's battle to overcome negative aspects of himself or herself, or to reconcile the conflict between the conscious and unconscious minds.

WATCH See **CLOCK**.

WATER Imagination, the unconscious, purity, and the source of life. Emerging from water represents a return to consciousness. Diving into water suggests exploration of the unconscious. A gushing faucet may connote male fertility.

WEDDING The unification of all aspects of self. The wedding feast, by association with food, signifies the reconciliation of factions.

WIND A light, warm wind represents a welcome change; a high wind or gale, a threatening or dreaded change. If the wind blows away the dreamer's house or possessions, this may be a warning of self-destructive or tempestuous impulses.

WITCH In childhood dreams, witches can represent any frightening aspects of the child's parents or other figures of authority, such as teachers. In adult dreams, witches represent negative aspects of the self which the dreamer is trying to come to terms with and ultimately break free from.

WOOD See **FOREST**.

WORKPLACE Often the setting for anxiety dreams, perhaps suggesting that the dreamer is not handling work pressures effectively or that he or she feels unsettled or unfulfilled at work. A dream of an overbearing boss may signify that the dreamer feels that his or her ambitions are being stifled.

ZOO Different animals symbolize different aspects of the dreaming psyche. (See **ANIMAL**.) A zoo in which all animals are locked up together is, therefore, a metaphor for control over the various turbulent and potentially conflicting aspects of self. A zoo from which animals are escaping signifies that the dreamer feels unable to keep control of the distractions in his or her life, or of his or her emotions.